Maps Globes Graphs

Steck Vaughn

Level B

Writer
Henry Billings

Consultants

Marian Gregory
Teacher
San Luis Coastal Unified School District
San Luis Obispo, California

Gloria Sesso
Supervisor of Social Studies
Half Hollow Hills School District
Dix Hills, New York

Norman McRae, Ph.D.
Former Director of Fine Arts and Social
Studies
Detroit Public Schools
Detroit, Michigan

Edna Whitfield
Former Social Studies Supervisor
St. Louis Public Schools
St. Louis, Missouri

Marilyn Nebenzahl
Social Studies Consultant
San Francisco, California

Karen Wiggins
Director of Social Studies
Richardson Independent School District
Richardson, Texas

Check the Maps•Globes•Graphs Website to find more fun geography activities at home.
Go to www.HarcourtAchieve.com/mggwelcome.html

Harcourt Achieve
Rigby • Steck-Vaughn

www.HarcourtAchieve.com
1.800.531.5015

Acknowledgments

Cartography

Land Registration and Information Service
  Amherst, Nova Scotia, Canada
Gary J. Robinson
MapQuest.com, Inc.
R.R. Donnelley and Sons Company
XNR Productions Inc., Madison, Wisconsin

Photography Credits

COVER (globe, clouds) © PhotoDisc; p. 4 © Superstock; p. 5(t) © PhotoDisc; p. 5(b) © Corel Photo Studios; pp. 6 (both), 7(t) © PhotoDisc; p. 7(b) © Gale Zucker/Stock Boston; p. 8(t) © Superstock; p. 8(b) © PhotoDisc; p. 9(t) © James Carmichael/The Image Bank; p. 9(b) © PhotoDisc; pp. 16, 22, 30(t) Dale Kirksey; p. 30(b) NASA; p. 36 © PhotoDisc; pp. 44, 52 Gary Russ

Illustration Credits

Dennis Harms pp. 29, 50, 51; David Griffin pp. 14a, 14b, 14c, 14d, 58a, 58b, 58c, 58d, 59; Michael Krone p. 17; T.K. Riddle p. 18; Rusty Kaim p. 4

ISBN 0-7398-9102-2

Contents

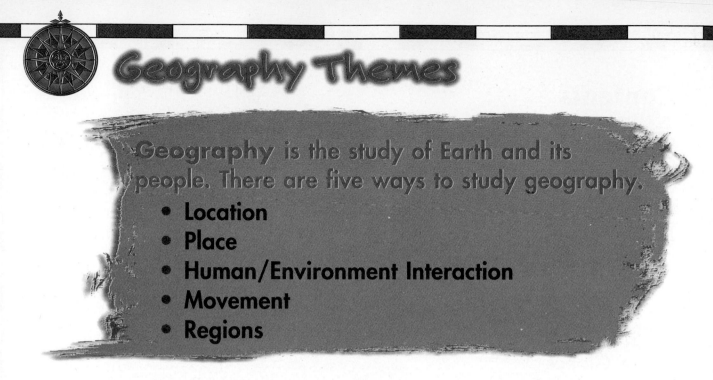

Geography Themes

Geography is the study of Earth and its people. There are five ways to study geography.

- **Location**
- **Place**
- **Human/Environment Interaction**
- **Movement**
- **Regions**

Location tells where something can be found. It tells what is nearby.

Frank lives by a lake. There are trees and mountains near his home.

1. Where is your home? What is it by?

_____

2. What is near your home?

_____

Place tells what a location is like.

Janis lives in a neighborhood with
  many houses.
She plays in the park on hot
  summer days.

3. How is this place different from where you live?

_____

_____

Human/Environment Interaction tells how people
use the land.

Sam lives on a farm.
His family grows corn
  and wheat.

4. How do people use the land where you live?

_____

_____

Human/Environment Interaction tells how people live with the weather. In warm weather people swim. People play baseball. In cold weather people wear hats, coats, and gloves.

There is a lot of rain where Chris lives.

5. What does Chris do in rainy weather?

_____

_____

Movement tells how people, goods, and ideas move from place to place.

Manny rides his bicycle to school.
His mother takes a bus to work.

6. How do toys get to the stores?

_____

Lewis learns new ideas from books.

7. Name other ways ideas move from place to place.

/

_____

_____

Regions are special areas that share something. Places in a mountain region all have mountains. Regions can be big or small. A neighborhood can be a region.

This picture shows Nathan's neighborhood.

8. How is Nathan's neighborhood like yours?

/

_____

_____

An **island** is a piece of land with water all around it.
A **lake** is a body of water with land all around it.
A **river** is a large stream of water that flows into a
larger body of water.
A **valley** is a low place between higher land.

hill

mountain

plain

ocean

A **hill** is land that rises above the land around it.
A **mountain** is land that rises higher than a hill.
A **plain** is flat land that is good for farming.
An **ocean** is the largest body of water on Earth.

Finding Water and Landforms

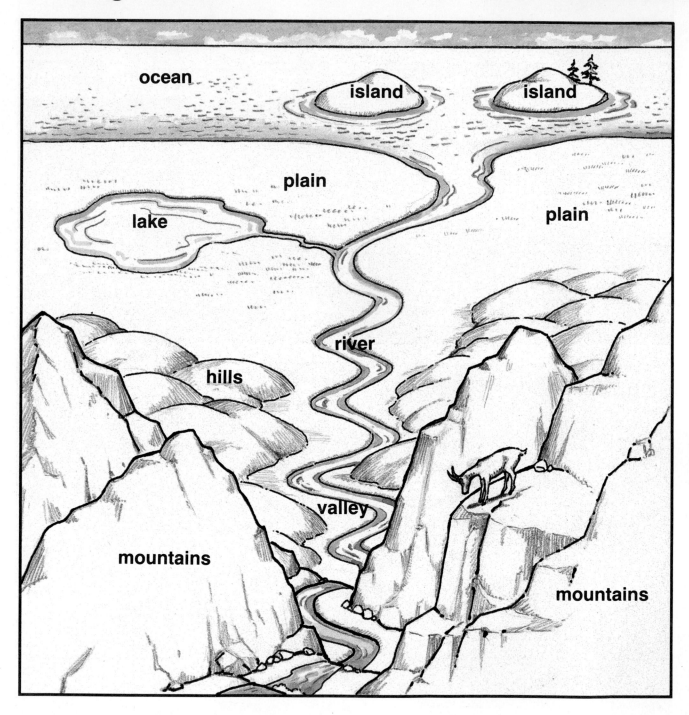

1. Read each word on the drawing.
2. Color the bodies of water blue.
3. Color the mountains, hills, and valley green.
4. Color the plains and islands yellow.

Name _____

Finding Water and Landforms

valley

1. Write each word from the list on the line where it belongs.

2. Color the river, lake, and ocean blue.

3. Color the mountains, hills, and valley green.

4. Color the plain and islands yellow.

Word List	
lake	mountains
plain	valley
river	ocean
hills	island

Finding Water and Landforms

Imagine you and your friend are riding horses. You ride down the trail to the beach.

1. Find the trail. Color it brown.
2. Write the name of each place you pass in the box where it belongs.

   mountains   lake   river
   valley   hills   plain

3. Draw a boat on the ocean.
4. Draw a tree on an island.

Skill Check

Words I Know island   plain   hill   mountain
ocean   river   lake   valley

1. What is land that is higher than a hill? _____

2. What is water with land all around it? _____

3. Draw a line to match each word with its picture.

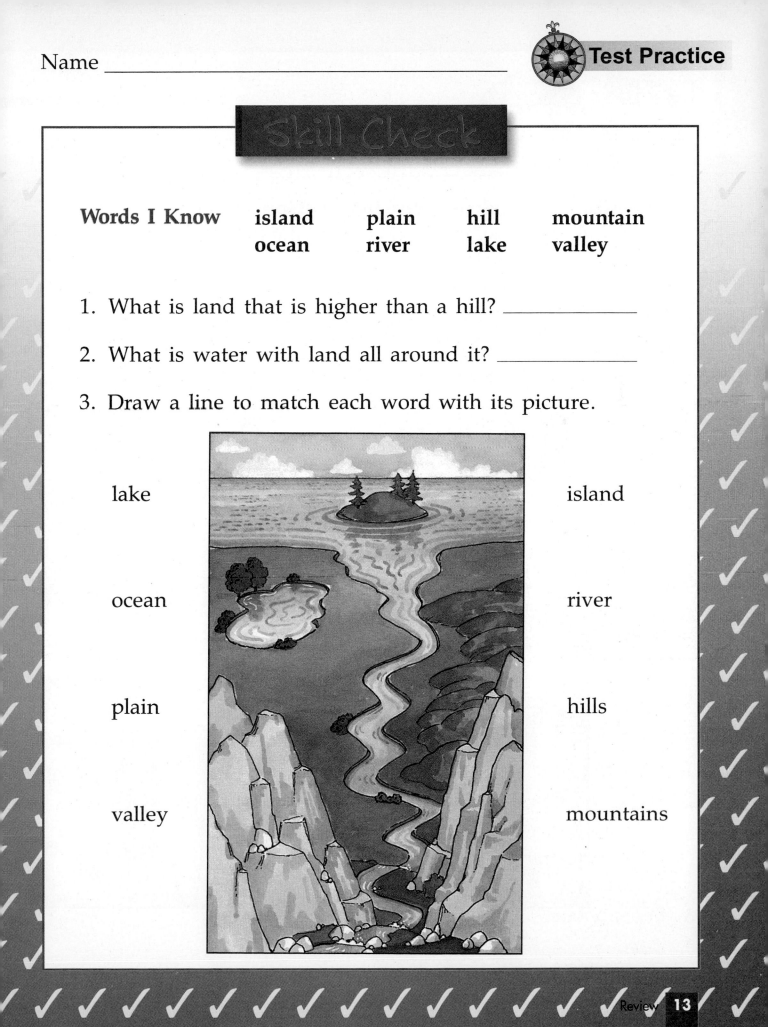

lake   island

ocean   river

plain   hills

valley   mountains

Human/Environment Interaction tells how people live, work, and play on Earth. Look at the pictures. They show people in different places. People do different things during the year. They make changes when it is hot or when it is cold. They change what they do. They change what they wear. Write what the people are doing below each picture.

1.

_____

2.

_____

3.

_____

4.

_____

People make changes to the land. In each box below, draw a picture showing how people change the land.

5. People build houses.

7. People build roads.

6. People plant gardens.

8. Draw a change in your neighborhood.

Maps and Map Keys

This **photo** shows a small town.
It was taken from above.
► What things can you see in the photo?

Name _____

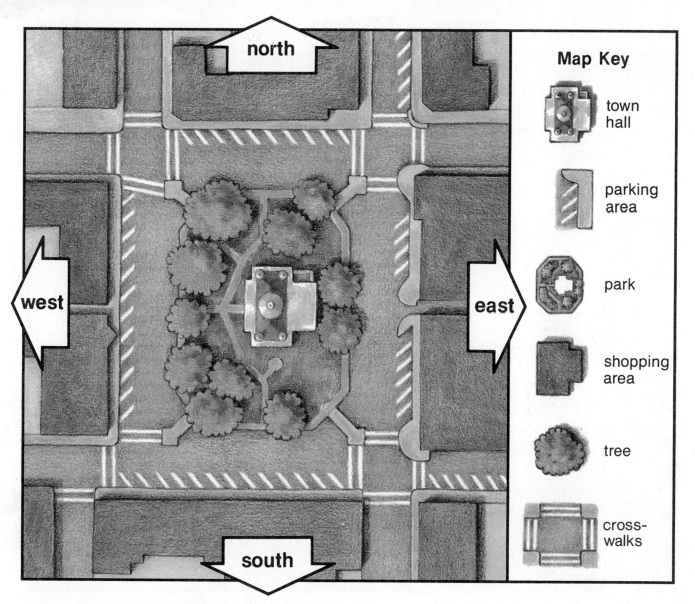

This map shows the same town.
A **map** is a drawing of a real place.
Symbols on the map stand for real things.
The **map key** tells what the symbols stand for.

Study the map key. Count the symbols on the map.
How many of each symbol are on the map?

town halls _____   parks _____   shopping areas _____

parking areas _____   trees _____   cross-walks _____

Reading Symbols on a Map

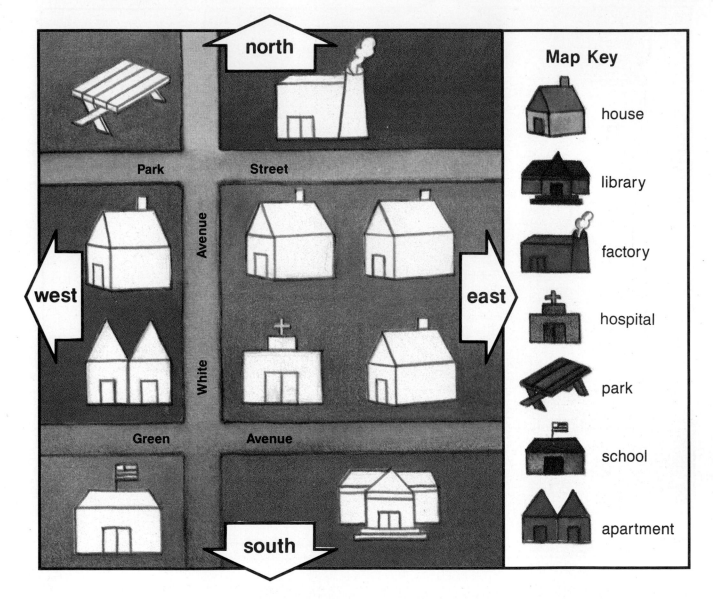

This map shows a neighborhood.

1. Circle each thing below that is closer to the school than to the park.

    hospital   apartment   library   factory

2. How many houses are there? _____

3. How many streets? _____

4. Color the symbols on the map to match the map key.

Name _____

Reading Symbols on a Map

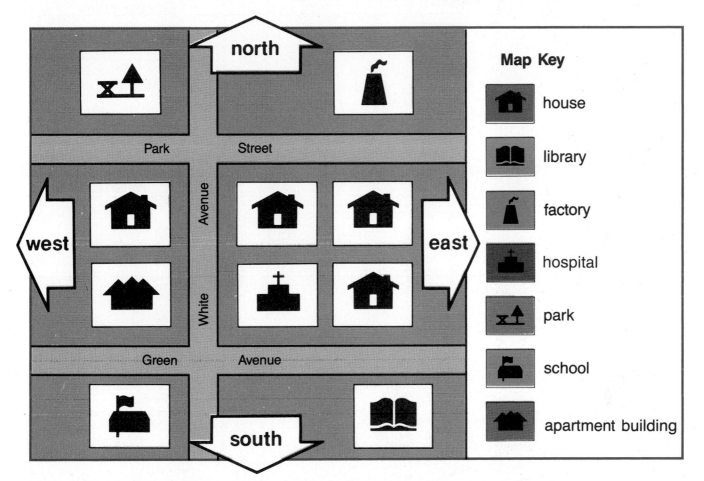

This map shows the same neighborhood.

1. Draw a red line showing how to get from the factory to the school.

2. What streets will you take? _____

_____

3. Name three things you pass. _____

_____   _____

4. Color the map to match the map key.

Finding Symbols on a Map

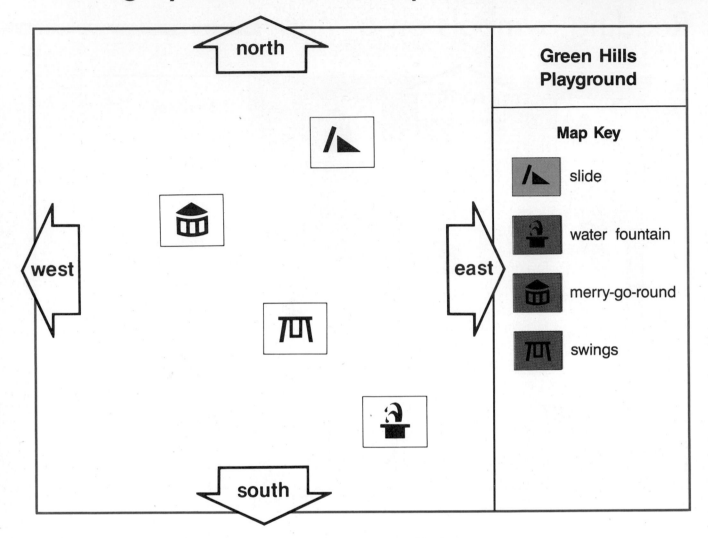

1. What is the name of this playground?

   _____

2. Circle the answers.

   The slide is nearest the

         merry-go-round.   water fountain.

   The swings are farthest from the

         slide.   water fountain.

3. Draw a water fountain next to the slide.

4. Color the map to match the map key.

Skill Check

Words I Know   map   symbol   map key   photo

Write the correct word next to each picture.

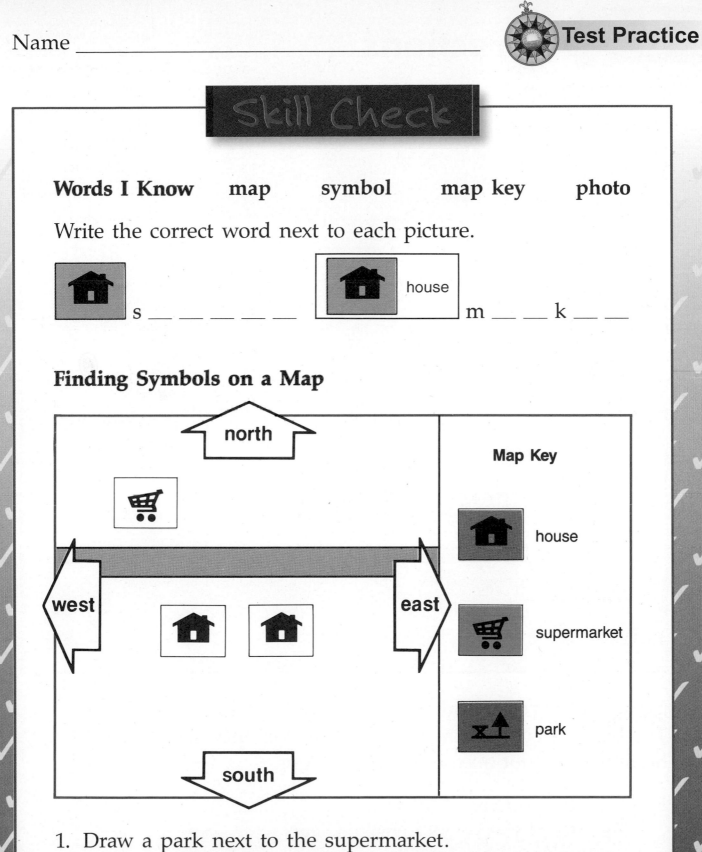

s _ _ _ _ _ _

house

m _ _ k _ _ _

Finding Symbols on a Map

north

west

east

south

Map Key

house

supermarket

park

1. Draw a park next to the supermarket.

2. Draw two houses at the bottom of the map.

3. Color the map to match the map key.

Directions

North, south, east, and west are four **directions**.
The boy is facing north. If the boy knows one direction,
he can figure out all the other directions.

Here is how you can do it:

> South is opposite north.
> When north is in front, south is behind you.
> When north is in front, east is to your right.
> West is opposite east. So west is to your left.

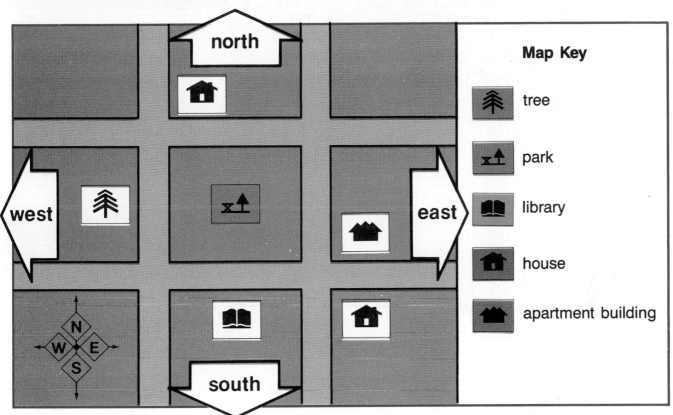

A **compass rose** is a symbol that shows direction.
It looks like this ⊹. Find it on the map.

The letters <u>N</u>, <u>S</u>, <u>E</u>, and <u>W</u> stand for north, south, east, and west. Find the letters on the compass rose.

1. Circle the compass rose on the map.

2. Name the opposite of each direction.

   north _____   east _____

   south _____   west _____

3. Color the house on the north yellow.

4. Color the library on the south blue.

5. Color the apartment on the east red.

6. Color the tree on the west green.

Finding Directions on a Map

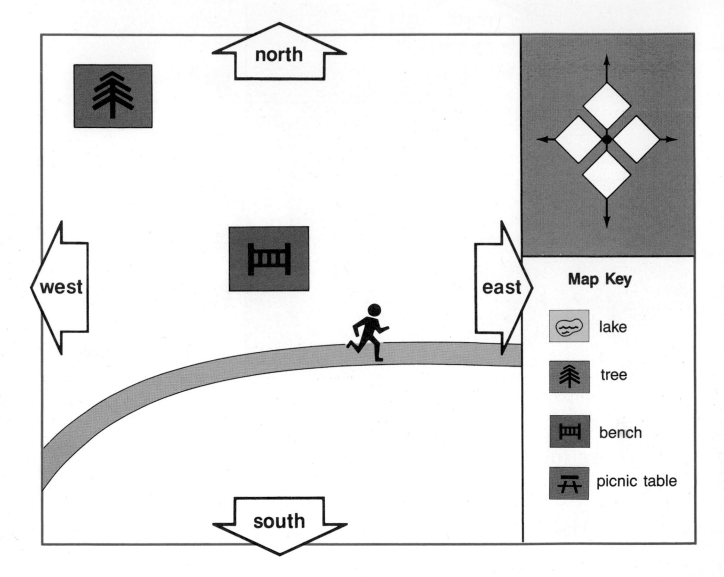

North is at the top of this map of a park.

1. Write the letters <u>N</u>, <u>S</u>, <u>E</u>, and <u>W</u> where they belong on the compass rose.

2. Draw a picnic table on the north. Color it red.

3. Draw a lake on the east. Color it blue.

4. Draw two trees on the south. Color them green.

5. Draw a bench on the west. Color it yellow.

6. In which direction is the person running? _____

Name _____

Finding Directions on a Map

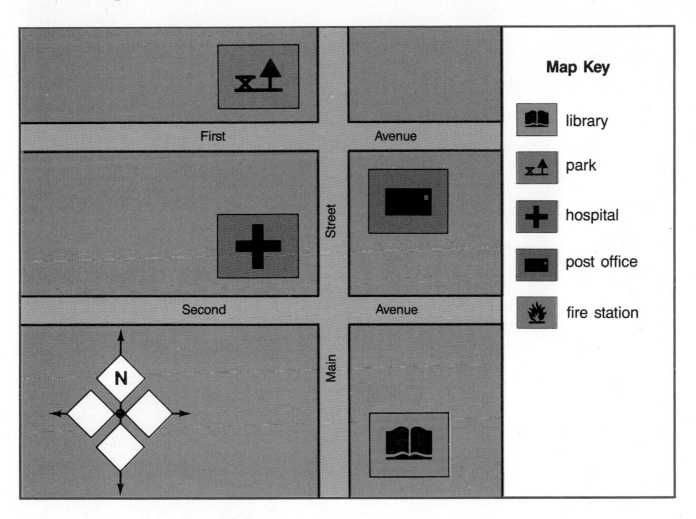

1. Write <u>S</u>, <u>E</u>, and <u>W</u> on the compass rose.

2. Write the direction that completes each sentence.

   The park is _____ of the hospital.

   The post office is _____ of the hospital.

   The library is _____ of the post office.

   The hospital is _____ of the post office.

3. Draw a fire station west of the hospital.

Finding Directions on a Map

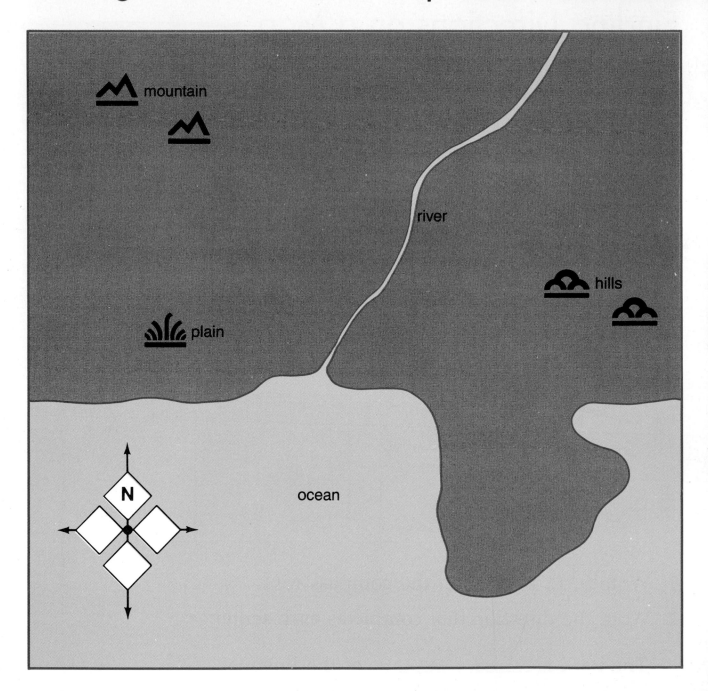

1. Write <u>S</u>, <u>E</u>, and <u>W</u> on the compass rose.
2. Draw a mountain east of the river. Use ⛰ .
3. Draw a plain south of the hills. Use 🌾 .
4. Draw a mountain north of the hills. Use ⛰ .
5. Draw two hills west of the river. Use ⛰ .

Skill Check

Words I Know   directions   north   east
                    compass rose   south   west

1. Which direction is opposite east? _____

2. Which direction is opposite north? _____

3. What is this symbol? _____

Finding Directions on a Map

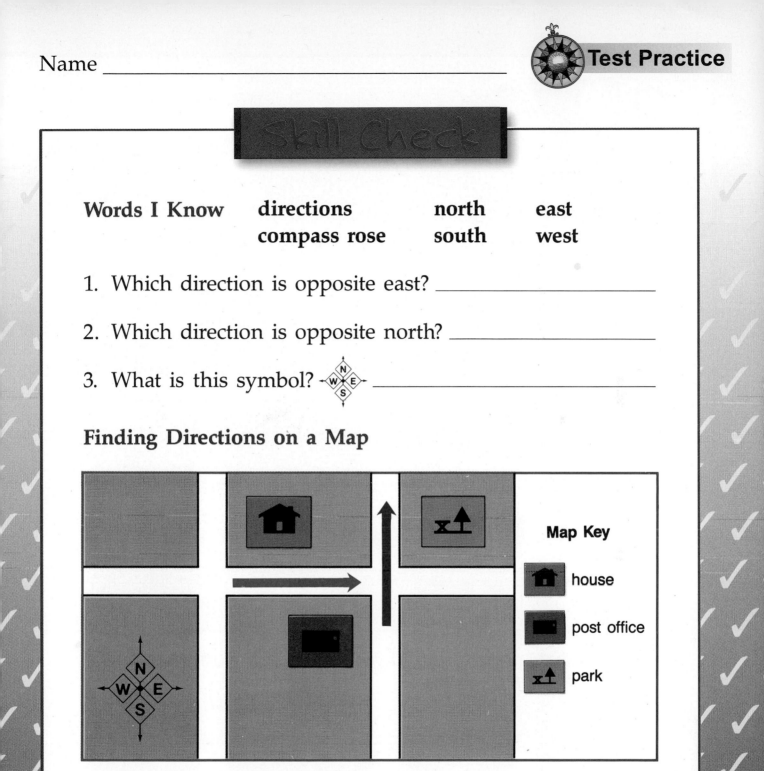

1. Draw a park west of the house.

2. Draw two houses east of the post office.

3. In which direction is the blue arrow pointing? _____

4. In which direction is the red arrow pointing? _____

Movement means how people, goods, and ideas get from one place to another. Highways move people and goods from place to place.

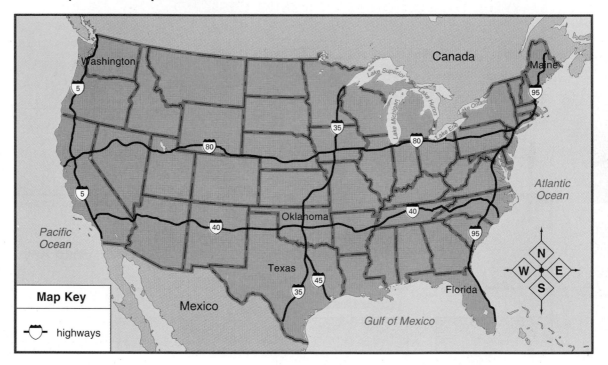

1. What highway could you take to go from Maine to Florida?

_____

2. What highways could a truck use to take apples from Washington to Oklahoma?

_____

3. What three highways go through Texas?

_____

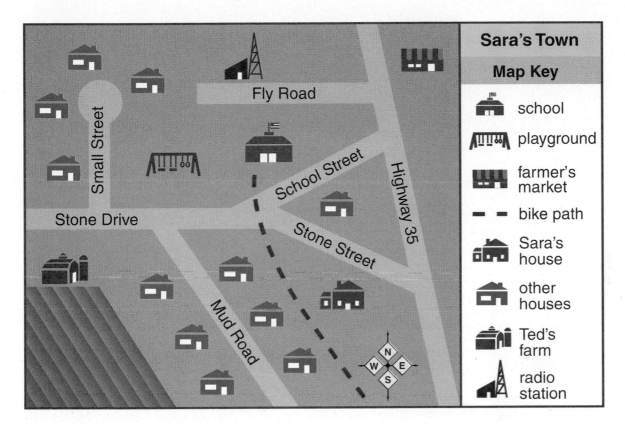

4. How can Sara get to school?

_____

_____

5. Ted grows corn on his farm. What streets and highways can he use to get his corn to the farmer's market?

_____

Ideas also move from place to place in Sara's town. Television is one way ideas move from place to place.

6. What are other ways that ideas move in Sara's town?

_____

4 Globes

The small photo shows Earth. It was taken from out in space.

The large photo shows a **globe**. A globe is a model of Earth. It is round like Earth.

Blue always stands for water. The oceans are the largest bodies of water. On this globe green stands for land. On other globes land can be other colors. **Continents** are the largest landforms.

► Find the globe in your classroom. What color is the land?

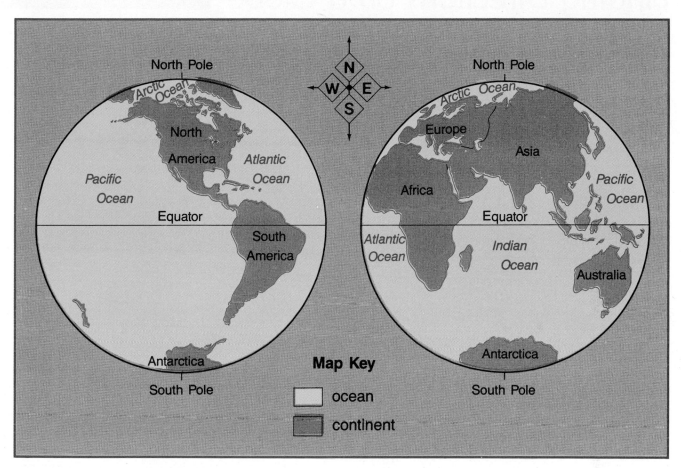

The globe is round like a ball. You can't see the whole thing at once. Here are both sides of one globe. Count the seven continents and four oceans. Earth is mostly covered by water.

The Seven Continents			
North America	Australia	Europe	Antarctica
South America	Africa	Asia	
The Four Oceans			
Pacific Ocean		Indian Ocean	
Atlantic Ocean		Arctic Ocean	

Can you see the line drawn around the center of the globe? This line is the **Equator**. It is an imaginary line that divides Earth in half.

Finding Directions on a Globe

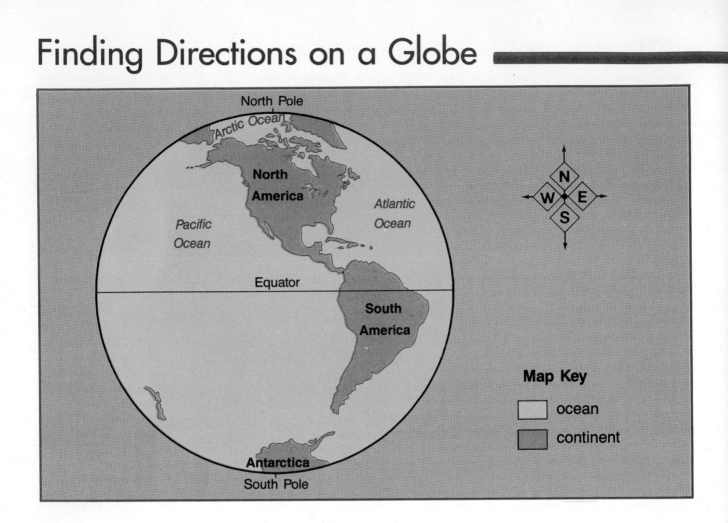

1. Find the Equator. Put an **X** on it.
2. Which continent is north of the Equator?

   _____

3. Which continent does the Equator pass through?

   _____

4. Which ocean is east of the two continents?

   _____

5. Which ocean is west of the two continents?

   _____

Name _____

Mapping a Globe

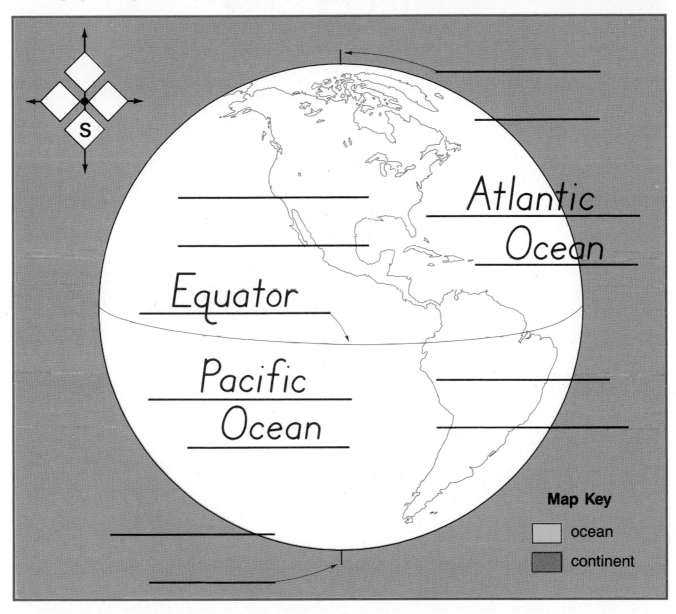

Atlantic Ocean

Equator

Pacific Ocean

Map Key

☐ ocean

■ continent

1. Complete the compass rose.

2. Write these names on the globe where they belong.
   North America   South Pole
   South America   North Pole

3. Color the continents to match the map key.

4. Color the oceans to match the map key.

Finding Directions on Globes

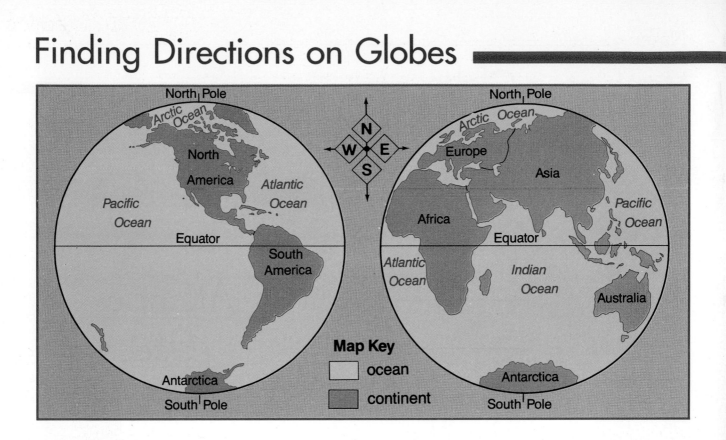

Study the map.
Find all seven continents. Find the four oceans.

1. Which continents are only north of the Equator?

_____   _____

_____

2. Which continents are only south of the Equator?

_____   _____

3. Which continents are north **and** south of the Equator?

_____   _____

4. Which ocean is east of Africa? _____

5. Which ocean is west of North America? _____

Name _____

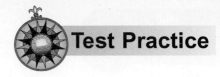
Skill Check

Words I Know   globe   continent   ocean

Write the correct word next to each picture.

 _____   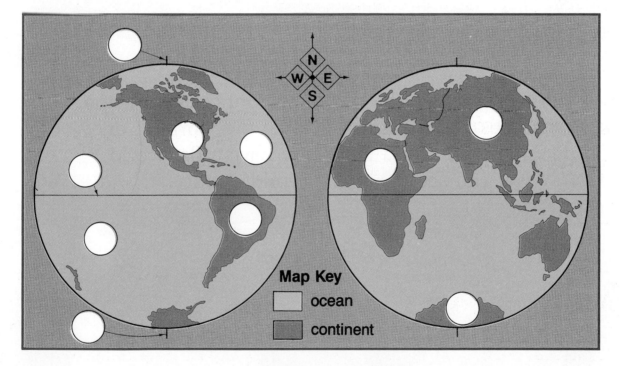 _____

Mapping a Globe

Map Key
☐ ocean
☐ continent

Write the number of each place on the map where it belongs.

① Equator   ⑤ North America   ⑨ Pacific Ocean
② North Pole   ⑥ South America   ⑩ Antarctica
③ South Pole   ⑦ Africa
④ Asia   ⑧ Atlantic Ocean

When you look at a globe you can see only one side at a time. Sometimes you want to see all of the world at once. If you peel the paper off a globe you have a flat world map. Now you can see the whole world at once.

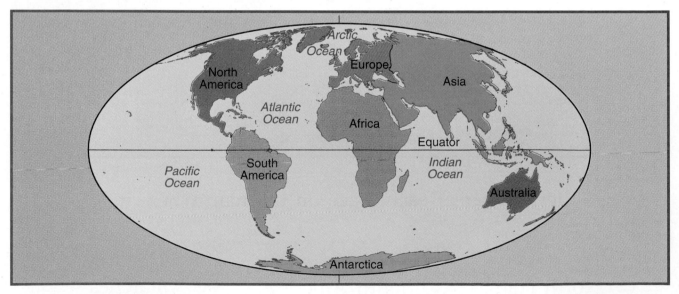

What continents can you see on this map that you can't see on the globes? What ocean can you see on this map that you can't see on the globes? How else are they different?

Name _____

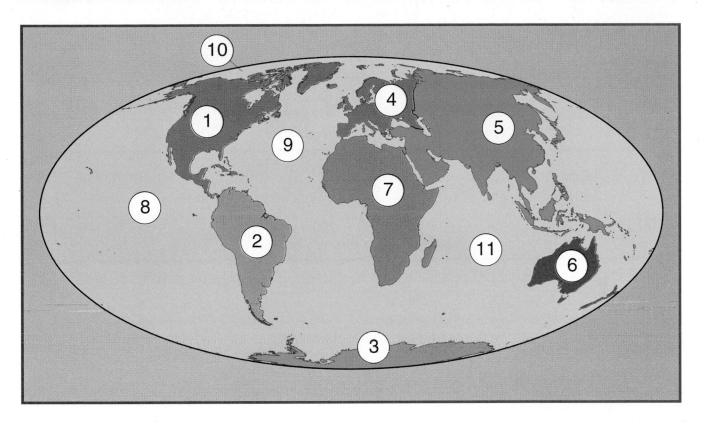

This map shows all seven continents and four oceans.

Write the continent and ocean names on these lines.

Continents

① _____

② _____

③ _____

④ _____

⑤ _____

⑥ _____

⑦ _____

Oceans

⑧ _____

⑨ _____

⑩ _____

⑪ _____

Finding Continents and Oceans

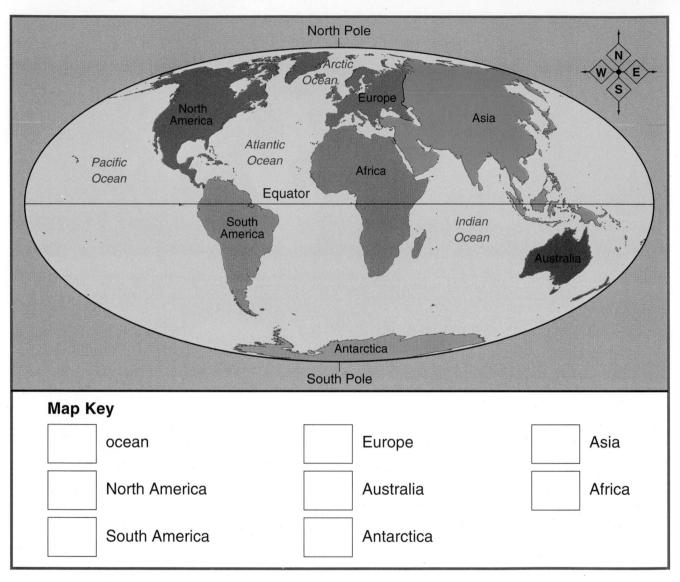

Map Key

☐ ocean

☐ North America

☐ South America

☐ Europe

☐ Australia

☐ Antarctica

☐ Asia

☐ Africa

This map shows the world's continents and oceans.

1. Color the map key to match the map.

2. Name two continents west of the Atlantic Ocean.

_____   _____

3. Name two continents south of Europe.

_____   _____

Name _____

Finding Continents and Oceans

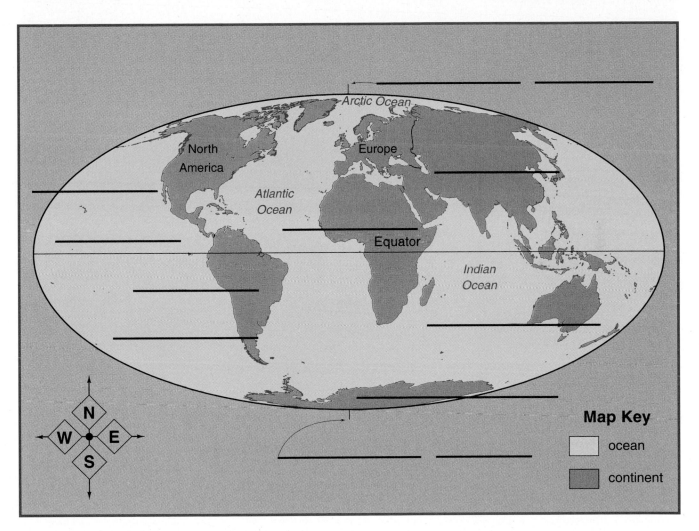

1. Write these names on the map where they belong.
   South America   Australia   North Pole
   Asia   Antarctica   South Pole
   Africa   Pacific Ocean

2. Name two continents that touch the Indian Ocean.

   _____   _____

3. Name two continents that touch the Atlantic Ocean.

   _____   _____

Finding Directions on a World Map

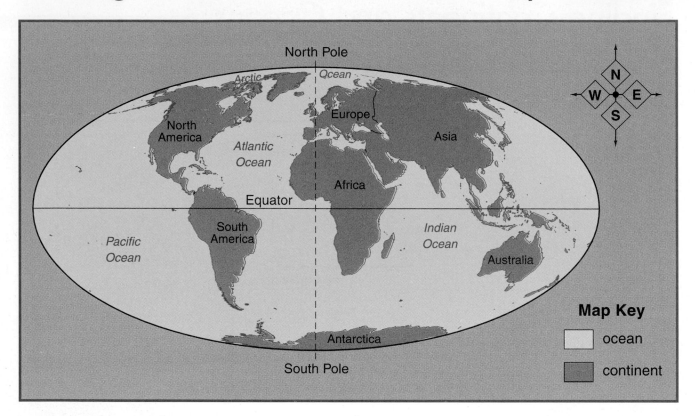

1. Find the Equator. Put an **X** on it.

2. Are these places <u>north</u> or <u>south</u> of the Equator?

   Antarctica _____   Australia _____

   North America _____   Europe _____

   Arctic Ocean _____   Asia _____

3. Finish the line between the North and South Poles.

4. Are these places <u>east</u> or <u>west</u> of the line you drew?

   South America _____   Asia _____

   Australia _____   Indian Ocean _____

   North America _____   Atlantic Ocean _____

Skill Check

Finding Places on a Map

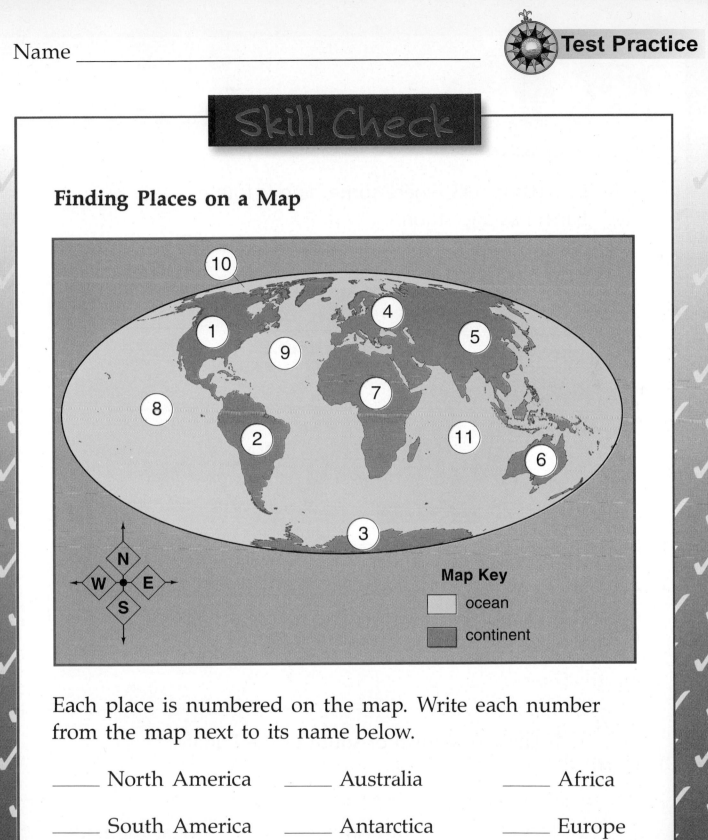

Map Key
- ☐ ocean
- ☐ continent

Each place is numbered on the map. Write each number from the map next to its name below.

____ North America   ____ Australia   ____ Africa

____ South America   ____ Antarctica   ____ Europe

____ Atlantic Ocean   ____ Indian Ocean   ____ Asia

____ Pacific Ocean   ____ Arctic Ocean

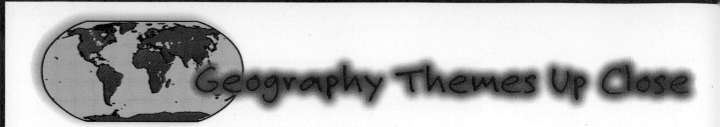
Location tells where something is found. Every place on Earth has a location.

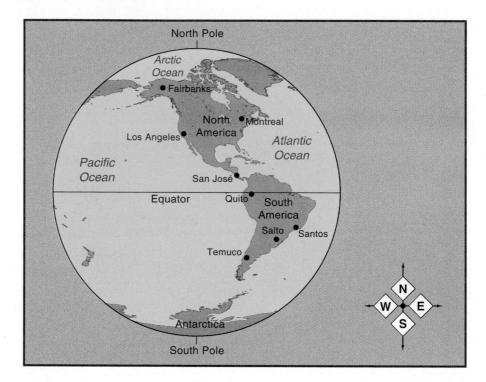

1. Find the city of Fairbanks. On what continent is it located?

   _____

2. Is Fairbanks north or south of the Equator?

   _____

3. This city is in South America. It is very near the Equator. Name the city.

   _____

A **grid** is made of lines that cross to make squares. A grid on a map helps you find a place. Look at the grid on the world map below.

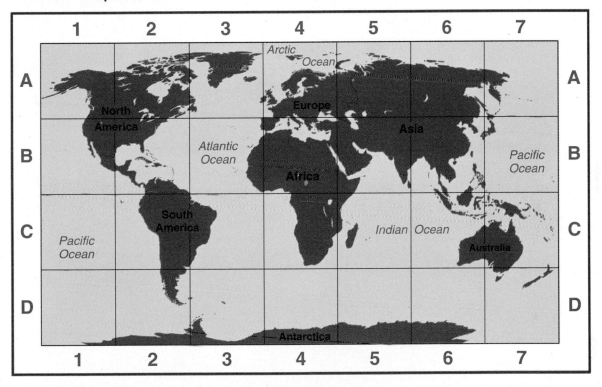

4. What continent is in square B-1?

_____

5. What ocean is in square A-4?

_____

6. What continent is in square C-7?

_____

7. What ocean is in C-5 and C-6?

_____

Can you see North America on this globe? North America has three large countries. They are Canada, Mexico, and the United States.

Can you see the edges or lines around each country? These are called **boundaries**. Boundaries show the end of one place and the beginning of another.

Name _____

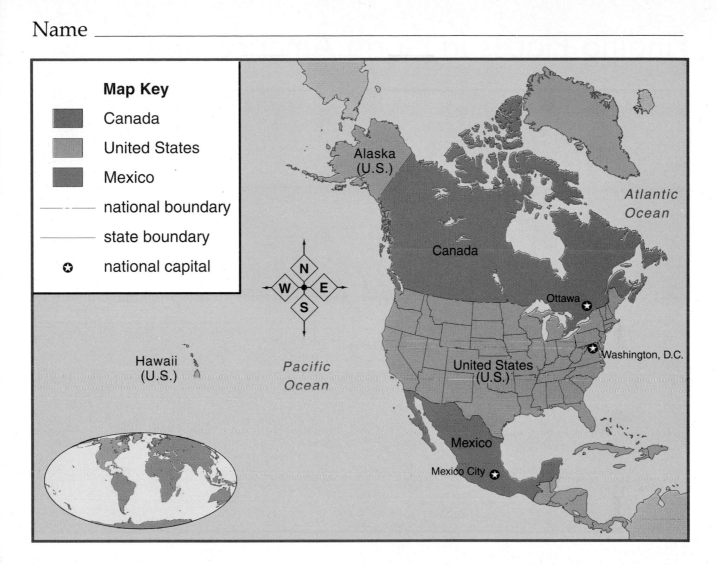

The small map shows where North America is in the world. The large map shows North America by itself.

Find the United States on the map. It is divided into 50 different states. A **state boundary** is shown with a solid black line. Alaska and Hawaii are states that are away from the rest of the United States. Find Alaska and Hawaii on the map. Circle them.

Canada is the country north of the United States. Mexico is the country south of the United States. Each country, or nation, has one capital city. The map key shows the symbols for a **national boundary** and a **national capital**. Circle one example of each symbol on the map.

Finding Places in North America

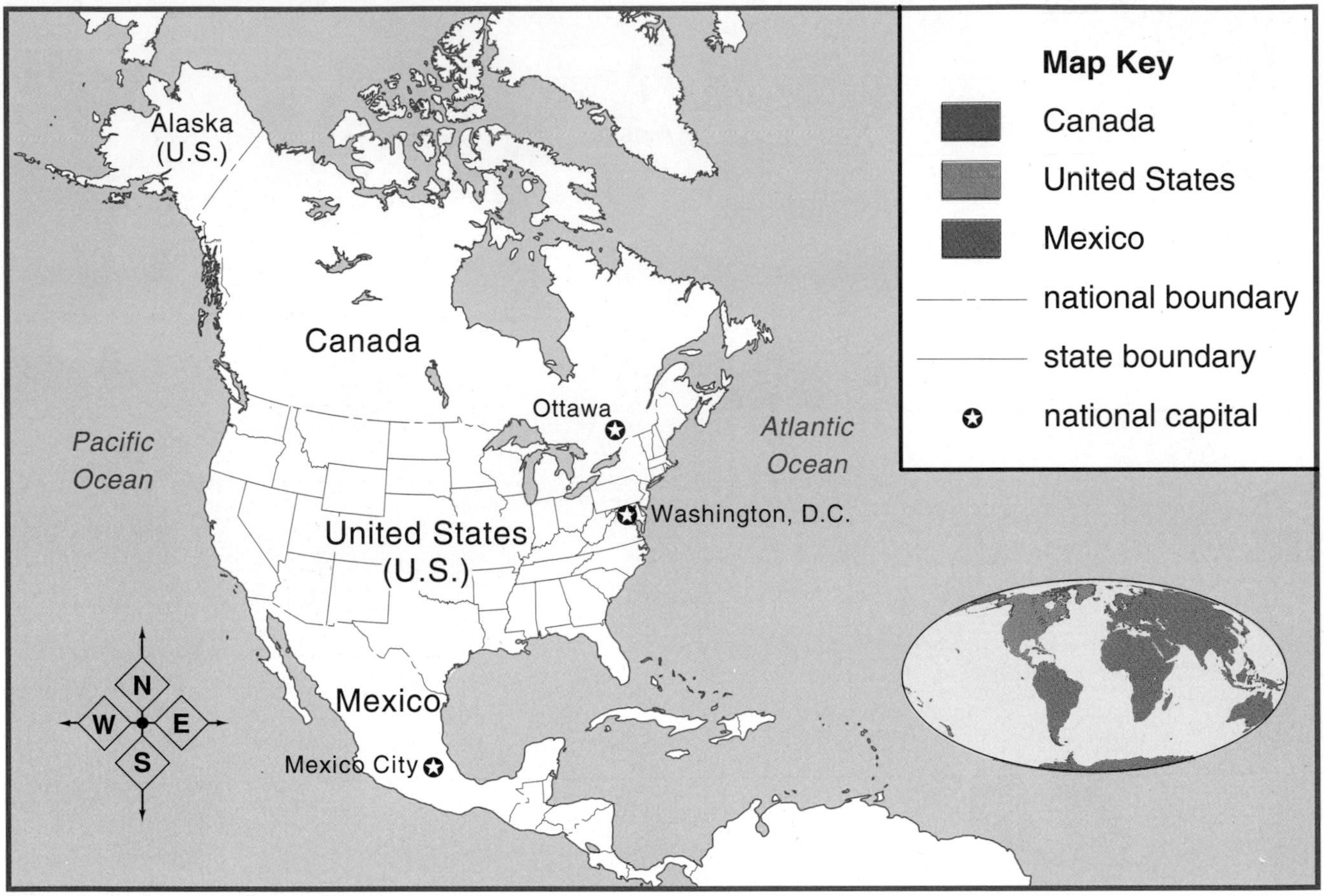
Map Key
Canada
United States
Mexico
national boundary
state boundary
national capital
Alaska (U.S.)
Canada
Ottawa
Pacific Ocean
Atlantic Ocean
Washington, D.C.
United States (U.S.)
Mexico
Mexico City
N
W
E
S

1. Color the United States green. Alaska and Hawaii are part of the U.S. Hawaii is not part of North America.
2. Color Canada yellow.
3. Color Mexico orange.
4. What is the capital of Mexico? ____________________
5. What is the capital of Canada? ____________________
6. What is the capital of the U.S.? ____________________
7. Circle the ocean name that is east of North America.
8. Put an **X** on the ocean name that is west of North America.

Name _____

Finding Places in North America

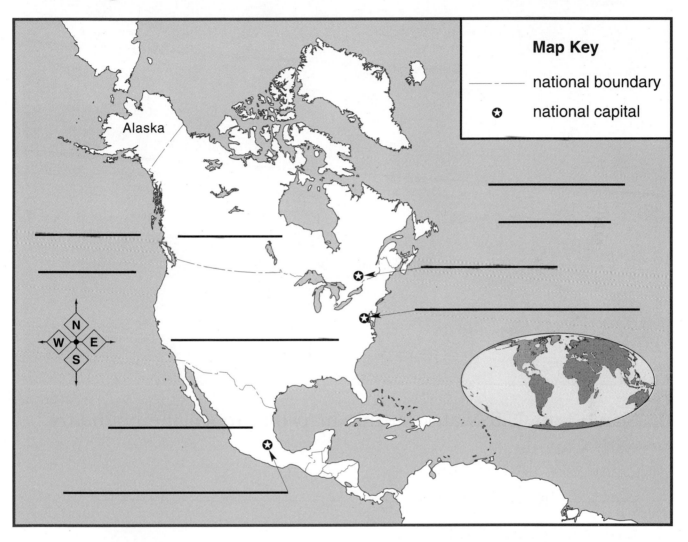

1. Write these names on the map where they belong.
   Atlantic Ocean   Mexico   United States
   Pacific Ocean   Canada   Washington, D.C.
   Mexico City   Ottawa

2. Draw a green line to show the boundaries between
   the U.S. and Canada. Remember that Alaska
   is part of the U.S.

3. Draw an orange line to show the boundary between
   the U.S. and Mexico.

Finding Boundaries

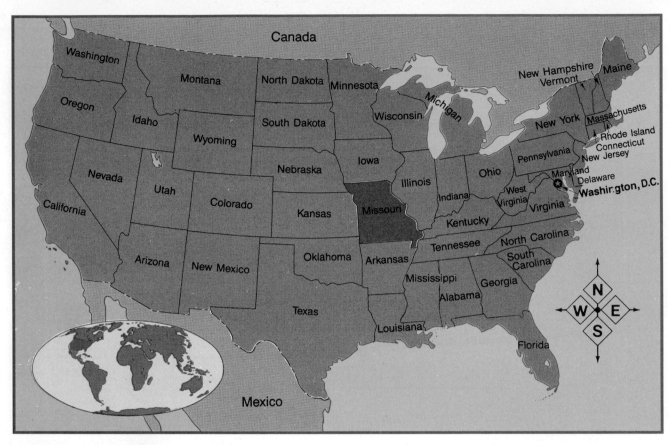

1. Name four U.S. states on this map that touch the boundary with Canada.

   _____   _____

   _____   _____

2. Name two states that touch the boundary with Mexico.

   _____   _____

3. Name one state that touches each side of Missouri.

   north _____   east _____

   south _____   west _____

Name _____

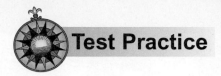

Skill Check

Words I Know **boundary**   **state boundary**
            national boundary **national capital**

Draw the symbols for:

[   ]   [   ]   [   ]

national boundary   state boundary   national capital

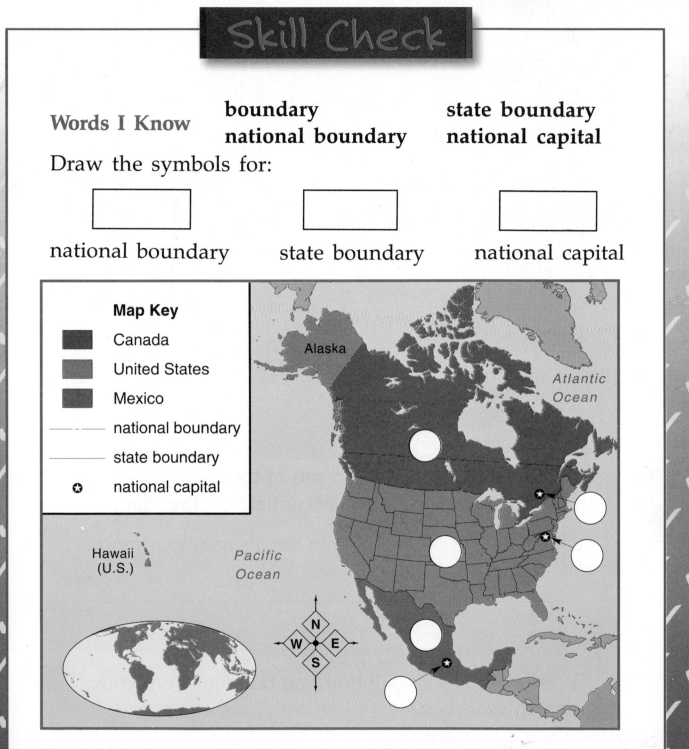

Map Key

Canada

United States

Mexico

— · — national boundary

——— state boundary

⊛ national capital

Alaska

Atlantic Ocean

Hawaii (U.S.)

Pacific Ocean

N W E S

Write the number of each place on the map where it belongs.

① Canada   ③ Mexico   ⑤ Washington, D.C.
② United States   ④ Ottawa   ⑥ Mexico City

Place tells what a location is like. It tells what makes a location special.

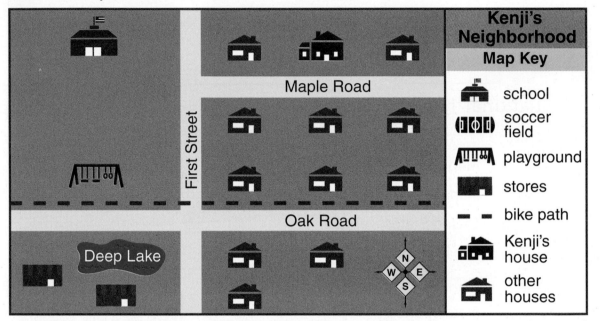

1. There is a soccer field north of the playground. It is south of the school. Draw a soccer field on the map.

2. Name two other things in Kenji's neighborhood.

_____

_____

3. How is Kenji's neighborhood different from your neighborhood?

_____

_____

_____

Place has things from nature like trees and rivers. Place also has things like houses that people build.

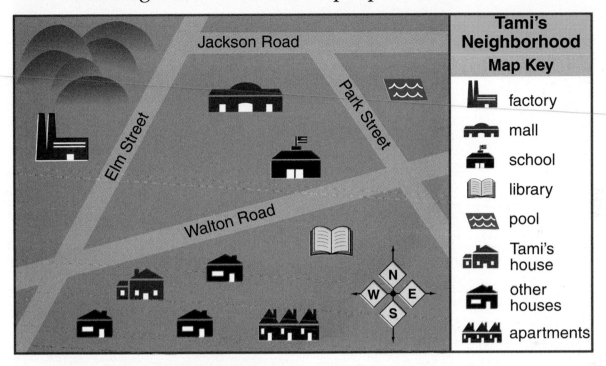

4. There are apartments south of the mall. Draw the apartments on the map.

5. The pool is east of the mall. Is the pool from nature or did people build it?

_____

6. Find the hills on the map. Mark an **N** on them if they are from nature. Mark a **P** if people made them.

7. What things in the neighborhood did people build?

_____

_____

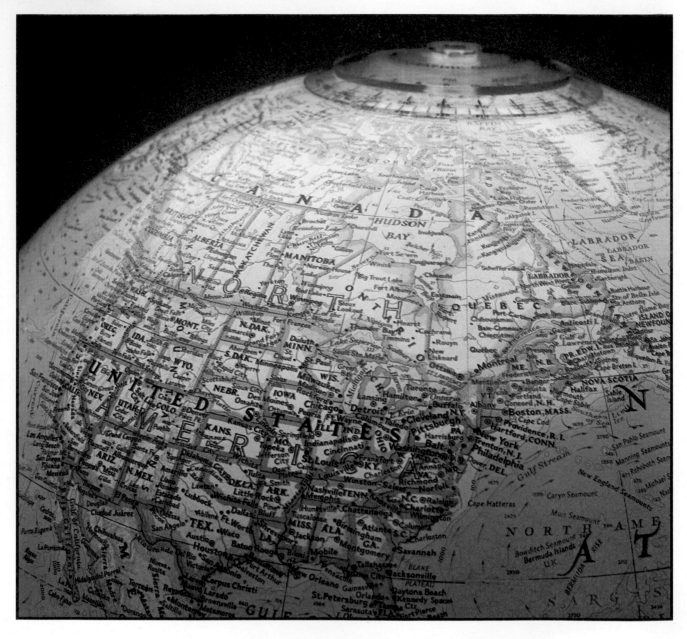

The words on a globe are called **labels**. The labels name the places on the globe.

Continents and oceans are the largest places. They have the biggest labels. Find the label for North America.

Countries, states, cities, and lakes are smaller places. They have smaller labels. Find the labels for United States, Canada, Ohio, Washington, D.C., and Lake Superior on the globe.

Name _____

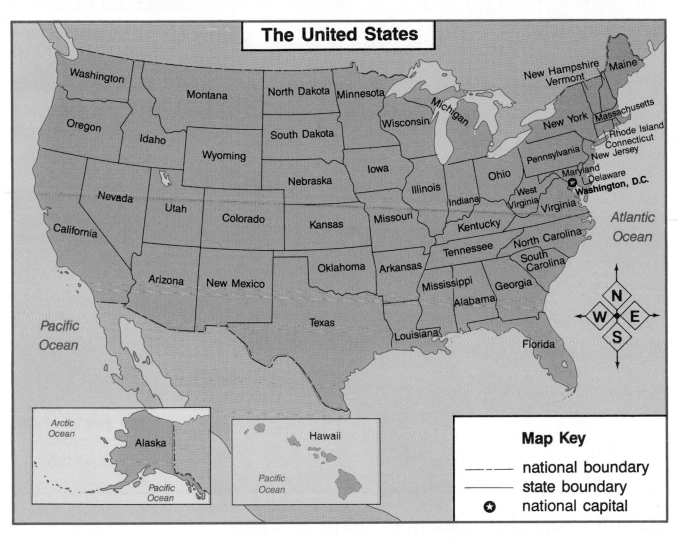

This map has a **title** or name. The title tells you what you are looking at. The title has the biggest, darkest letters on the map.

Alaska and Hawaii are far away from the other 48 states. They appear in special boxes called **inset maps**. Now you can see all 50 states on one page.

1. Circle one inset map.

2. Circle the map title.

3. Draw a box around your state's label.

4. Draw a line under the ocean labels.

Reading Map Labels

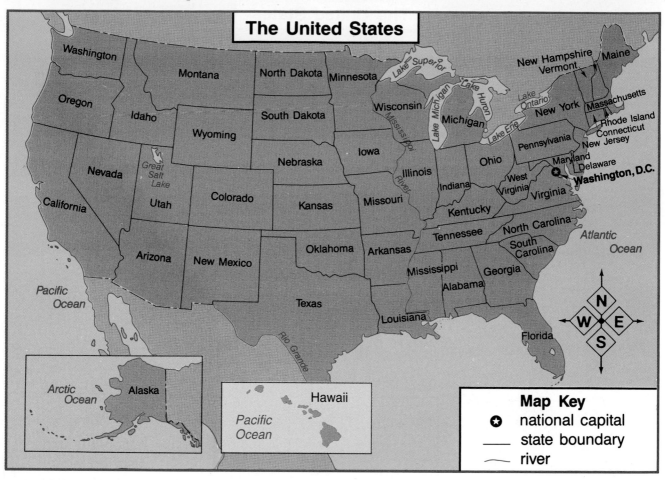

The United States

Washington

Montana

North Dakota

Minnesota

Lake Superior

New Hampshire
Vermont

Maine

Oregon

Idaho

South Dakota

Wisconsin

Lake Michigan

Lake Huron

Michigan

Lake Ontario

Lake Erie

New York

Massachusetts

Rhode Island
Connecticut
New Jersey

Wyoming

Mississippi

Pennsylvania

Nevada

Great
Salt
Lake

Nebraska

Iowa

Illinois

Ohio

Maryland

Delaware

Washington, D.C.

California

Utah

Colorado

Kansas

Missouri

Indiana

West
Virginia

Virginia

Kentucky

Tennessee

North Carolina

Atlantic
Ocean

Arizona

New Mexico

Oklahoma

Arkansas

South
Carolina

Pacific
Ocean

Mississippi

Georgia

Alabama

Texas

Louisiana

Rio Grande

River

Florida

N
W E
S

Arctic
Ocean

Alaska

Hawaii

Pacific
Ocean

Map Key
⊛ national capital
___ state boundary
⌒ river

Find the river that goes from north to south.
It is the Mississippi River.
The Mississippi River is a boundary for many states.

1. Name six states with a boundary formed by a river.

_____   _____

_____   _____

_____   _____

2. What is the title of the map? _____

Name _____

Finding Places in the United States

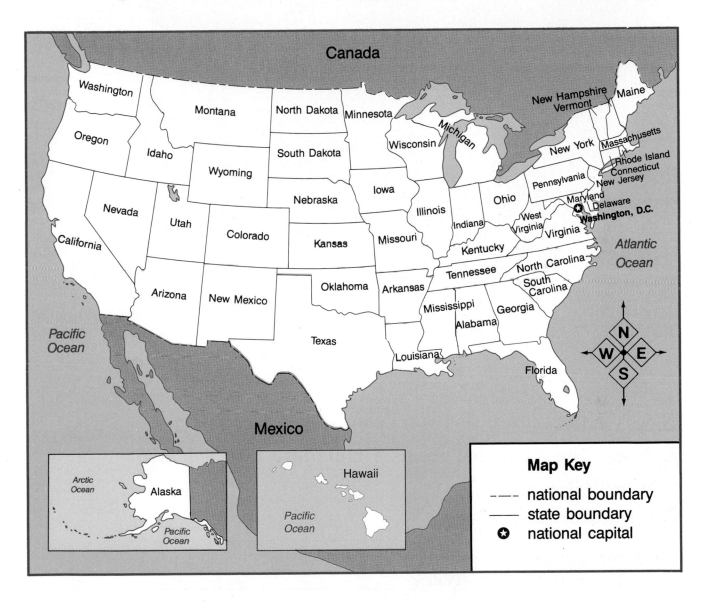

1. Make up a title for the map. _____

2. Find your state on the map. Circle it.

3. Find two countries outside the U.S. Name them.

_____   _____

4. Color the states touching Canada yellow.
   Color the states touching Mexico brown.

Finding Water and Landforms

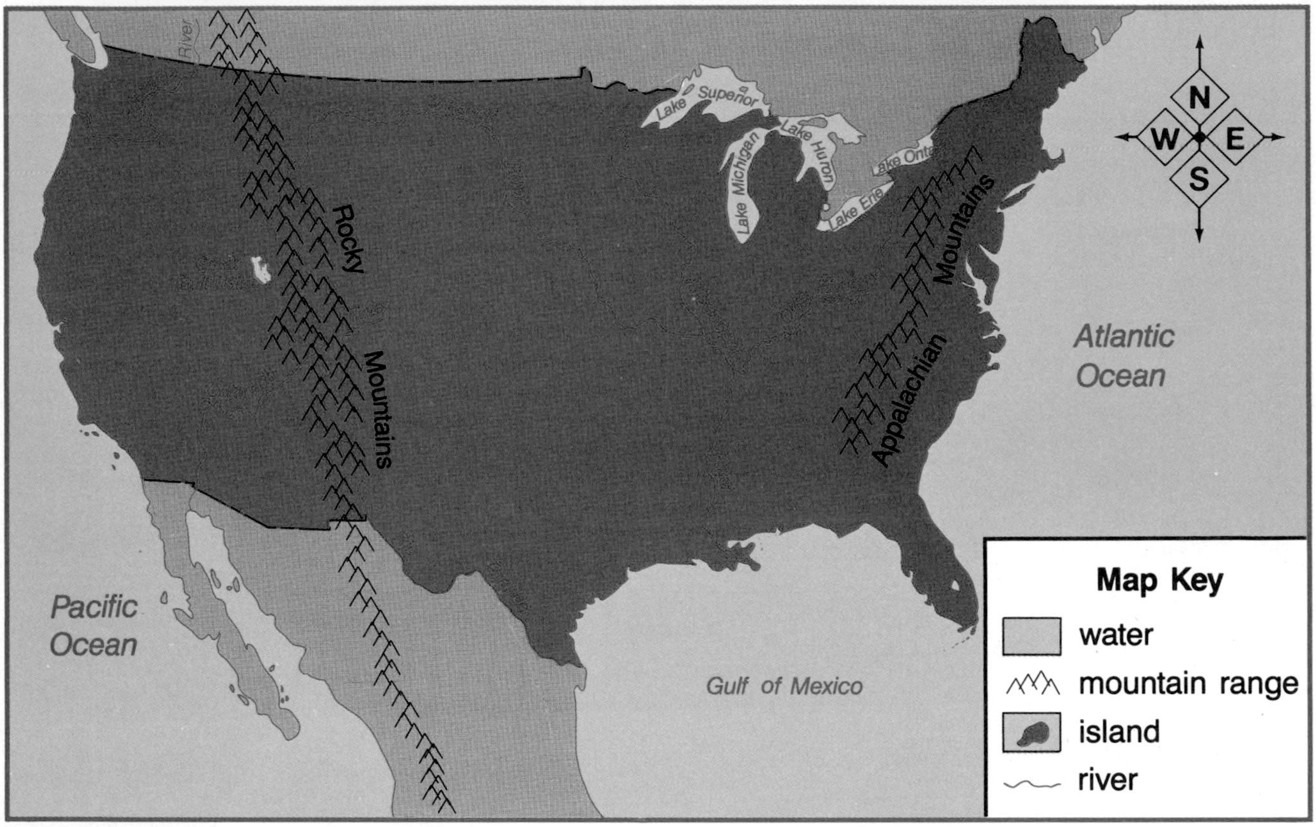
Lake Superior
Lake Michigan
Lake Huron
Lake Erie
Lake Ontario
Rocky Mountains
Appalachian Mountains
Atlantic Ocean
Pacific Ocean
Gulf of Mexico
N
S
E
W
Map Key
water
mountain range
island
river

1. Circle the names of two oceans on the map.
2. Name the river that forms a boundary between two countries.

   ____

3. Name three other rivers. ______________________________

   ____

4. Name two lakes. ______________________________

   ____

5. Circle one mountain range on the map.

Name _____

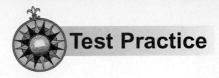

Skill Check

Words I Know label title inset map

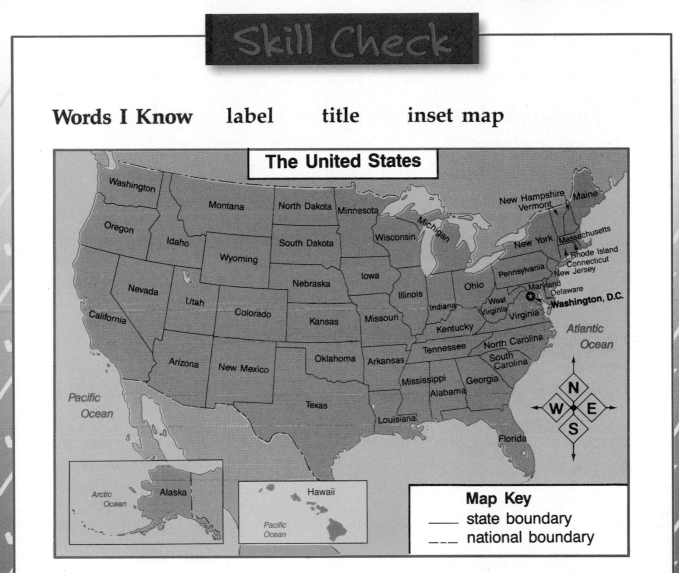

The United States

Washington
Montana
North Dakota
Minnesota
Oregon
Idaho
South Dakota
Wisconsin
Michigan
New Hampshire
Vermont
Maine
New York
Massachusetts
Rhode Island
Connecticut
New Jersey
Wyoming
Iowa
Nevada
Nebraska
Illinois
Ohio
Pennsylvania
Maryland
Delaware
Washington, D.C.
Utah
Colorado
Indiana
West Virginia
Virginia
California
Kansas
Missouri
Kentucky
Atlantic Ocean
Arizona
New Mexico
Oklahoma
Arkansas
Tennessee
North Carolina
South Carolina
Mississippi
Georgia
Alabama
Texas
Louisiana
Florida
Pacific Ocean

N
W • E
S

Alaska
Arctic Ocean
Hawaii
Pacific Ocean

Map Key
_____ state boundary
_ _ _ national boundary

1. Put an **X** on a label, a title, and an inset map.

2. Name the states shown in the inset maps.

_____ _____

3. Circle the places below that are labeled on the map.

oceans   mountains   continents

river   hills   lake

plains   states   national capital

Regions share something that makes them different from other places. A region can have the same kinds of plants. Regions can be big or small.

This is a **chart**. It shows facts in a way that is easy to read. This chart shows the kinds of plants and animals in three regions.

Regions	Plants	Animals
	trees, bushes, moss	goats, sheep, bears
	trees, grasses	deer, rabbits, squirrels, birds
	seaweeds	fish, shellfish, whales, dolphins

1. In which region does moss grow?

   _____

2. What animals live in plains regions?

   _____

3. What plants grow in ocean regions?

   _____

A neighborhood can be a region. A neighborhood has places for people to live, work, and play.

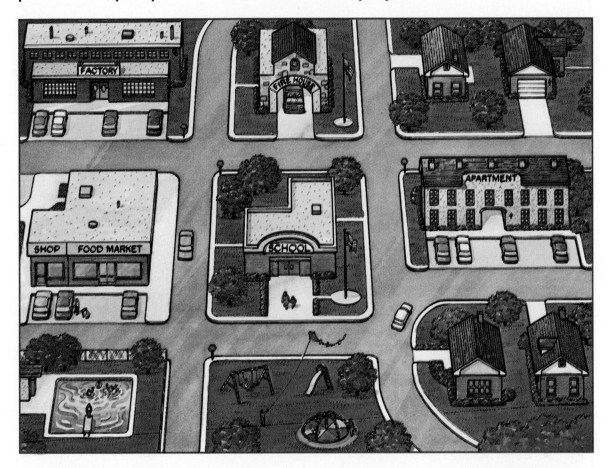

4. Find a place to live on the map. Mark an **X** below it.

5. Name a place in the neighborhood where people work.

_____

6. Find places to play. Which of these places do you have in your neighborhood?

_____

_____

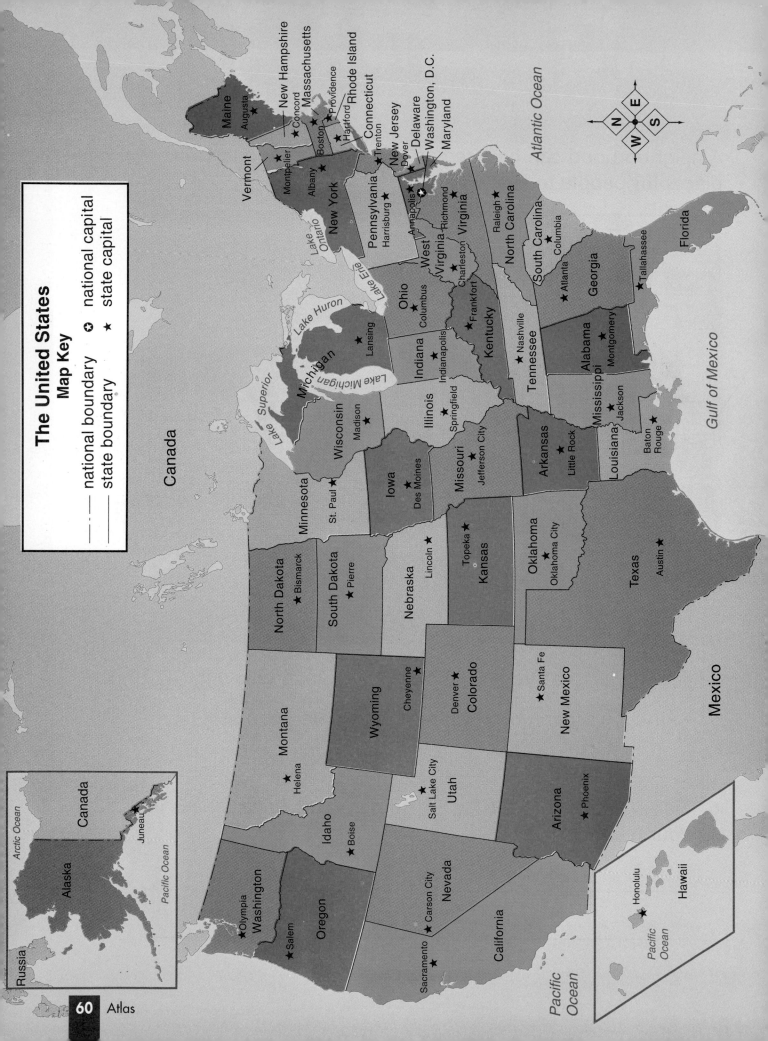

The United States
Map Key

national boundary
state boundary
⊛ national capital
★ state capital

Russia

Arctic Ocean

Canada

Alaska

Juneau ★

Pacific Ocean

Pacific Ocean

Honolulu
★

Hawaii

Mexico

Canada

Washington
Olympia ★

Oregon
Salem ★

Idaho
Boise ★

Montana
Helena ★

Wyoming
Cheyenne ★

North Dakota
★ Bismarck

South Dakota
★ Pierre

Minnesota
St. Paul ★

Nevada
Carson City ★

Utah
Salt Lake City ★

Colorado
Denver ★

Nebraska
Lincoln ★

Iowa
Des Moines ★

Wisconsin
Madison ★

Sacramento ★

California

Arizona
Phoenix ★

New Mexico
★ Santa Fe

Kansas
Topeka ★

Missouri
Jefferson City ★

Illinois
Springfield ★

Michigan
Lansing ★

Indiana
Indianapolis ★

Ohio
Columbus ★

Texas
Austin ★

Oklahoma
Oklahoma City ★

Arkansas
Little Rock ★

Tennessee
Nashville ★

Kentucky
Frankfort ★

West Virginia
Charleston ★

Mississippi
Jackson ★

Alabama
Montgomery ★

Louisiana
Baton Rouge ★

Gulf of Mexico

Georgia
Atlanta ★

South Carolina
Columbia ★

North Carolina
Raleigh ★

Virginia
Richmond ★

Florida
Tallahassee ★

Pennsylvania
Harrisburg ★

New York
Albany ★

Vermont
Montpelier ★

Maine
Augusta ★

New Hampshire
Concord ★

Massachusetts
Boston ★

Rhode Island
Providence ★

Connecticut
Hartford ★

New Jersey
Trenton ★

Delaware
Dover ★

Washington, D.C.
Annapolis ★
Maryland

Atlantic Ocean

Lake Superior

Lake Michigan

Lake Huron

Lake Erie

Lake Ontario

N
E
S
W

Arctic Ocean

Greenland

(U.S.)

Canada

Hudson
Bay

Pacific Ocean

Ottawa

Great
Lakes

United States

Washington, D.C.

Atlantic Ocean

N
W   E
S

Gulf of Mexico

Bahamas

U.S.
Virgin
Islands

Mexico

Cuba

Haiti

Puerto
Rico

Dominican
Republic

Jamaica

Mexico City

Belize

Caribbean Sea

Guatemala

Honduras

El Salvador

Nicaragua

Costa Rica

Panama

North America

The World

Pacific Ocean

Australia

Asia

Europe

Indian Ocean

Africa

Arctic Ocean

Antarctica

Atlantic Ocean

South America

North America

Equator

Pacific Ocean

N E W S

Glossary

boundary (p. 44) the dividing line on a map where one place begins and another place ends

capital city (p. 45) a place where laws are made for a state or country

chart (p. 58) facts shown in a way that is easy to read

compass rose (p. 23) a symbol that shows the directions: north, south, east, and west

continent (p. 30) the largest landforms. There are seven continents on Earth.

directions (p. 22) the four directions are north, south, east, and west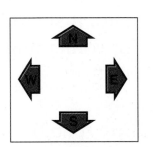

Equator (p. 31) the imaginary line around the middle of Earth

globe (p. 30) a model of Earth

grid (p. 43) lines that cross each other to make squares

hill (p. 9) land that rises above the land around it

human/environment interaction (pp. 5, 14) tells how people live, work, and play on Earth. It tells how people use the land.

inset map (p. 53) a special box on a main map with a smaller map inside

island (p. 8) land with water all around it

label (p. 52) a word that names a place on a map or a globe

lake (p. 8) a body of water with land all around it

location (p. 4, 42) tells where something is found on Earth

map (p. 17) a drawing of a real place. A map shows the place from above.

map key (p. 17) the guide that tells what the symbols on a map stand for

mountain (p. 9) land that rises higher than a hill

movement (p. 6, 28) how people, goods, and ideas get from one place to another

national boundary (p. 45) the dividing line on a map between nations or countries

national capital (p. 45) a place where laws are made for a nation or country

ocean (p. 9) the largest body of water on Earth

photo (p. 16) a picture made by a camera

place (p. 5, 50) tells what a location is like

plain (p. 9) flat land that is good for farming

regions (p. 7, 58) parts of Earth that are alike

river (p. 8) a large stream of water that flows into a larger body of water

state boundary (p. 45) the dividing line on a map between states

symbol (p. 17) a picture on a map. It stands for something real.

title (p. 53) the name of a map

valley (p. 8) a low place between higher land